The Wisdom of Solomon

Also Known As

The Book of Wisdom

The Book of Wisdom of Solomon Also Known As The Book of Wisdom

Copyright and related rights waived

Public Doman Dedication (see below)

Publishers Cataloging in Publication Data

The Book of Wisdom of Solomon Also Known As The Book of Wisdom

First Edition 2023

No Copyright

Table of Contents

Introduction

With the exception of early King James Versions and some Eastern Orthodox Versions, The Wisdom of Solomon also known as The Book of Wisdom has been omitted from Bibles we find today. Why is that? Is it not scripture? Is the book forged? Was the book not from antiquity? Was the book not written by an historical person? Does it not portray historical events? Does it not portray those who have dedicated their lives to the Supreme Being?

Let's take a look at these possible reasons and try to figure out why The Wisdom of Solomon has been excluded and ignored for centuries.

The Wisdom of Solomon was seemingly written somewhere between two hundred years before Christ to the First Century after Jesus' arrival.

According to many scholars, the book was written in Alexandria Greece during this time.

However, like many ancient texts, there is also the possibility that the book existed prior to this era, and perhaps was simply transcribed from Hebrew to Greek. A Hebrew text version has not been found, however.

It is obvious from the text itself that this is a dedicated follower of Moses and Solomon at the very least. There is also a distinct possibility that the text was originally written by Solomon. This possibility assumes the loss of the original manuscript during the tumultuous times of the 10th Century BCE and when the Greek translation appeared.

With regard to why the Wisdom of Solomon isn't in more Bibles, quite simply, the Protestant clergy did not accept this book as a canon – or part of the Bible. Subsequently they called the book Apocrypha simply because of the era of the book.

Apocrypha can have several meanings but it essentially refers to books that were not part of the ancient collection of Hebrew texts. They seemingly were written between the 2nd century BCE and the 4th century CE. The question in this regard is whether those dates are when the books were originally written, or whether they were written or passed down orally previous to their subsequent recorded writing.

There is now clear evidence, for example, from the Dead Sea Scrolls discovery, that books that were thought to have been written later in Greek or otherwise, did have Hebrew versions prior. This includes the Book of Enoch, which was found to have a Hebrew text older than later translations into Greek.

Indeed, it is not as if none of the ancient Hebrew texts have been lost or damaged in the many wars and fires that took place as the Israelites and Judeans battled their opponents, sometimes losing and subjected to expulsions and exoduses from their homelands. During these times of crises, many of the ancient scriptures were lost to history.

This could certainly apply to the Wisdom of Solomon, because after all, the text does reference historical events such as the Israelites' escape from Egypt and the crossing of the Red Sea. And there is certainly a first person reference throughout the text that appears to refer to Solomon.

Nonetheless, many scholars suggest that that the Greek version of the Wisdom of Solomon was written a Century or two prior to Jesus' arrival. They also suggest that the book was first written in Greek. Again, this comes from the notion that a Hebrew version of the book has not been found.

As you will find, the text can be divided into three potential parts. These include the reason for justice in human civilization; the need and benefits of wisdom; and how wisdom played a role in the history of the Israelites, especially during the time of Moses.

The book also documents a period of history when the Israelites escaped the heavy handed rule of the Egyptians and were guided into the desert and through the Red Sea as they were escaping the Egyptian army.

Note that most translations utilize draft text, as though this scripture was written as a historical ledger.

But it is obvious from the text is that this was written as prose. Like much of the Bible, the test of the Wisdom of Solomon is a recording of lengthy but beautiful prose.

This translation honors that approach and has attempted to translate the text into a modern English translation of the prose.

So what does Solomon have to do with this chapter? Did Solomon write it?

It does not seem to be a work of Solomon's. But it could be a contemporary of Solomon or someone dedicated to Solomon that wrote it.

Nonetheless, this text does illuminate the reality that Solomon exemplified what is contained in these texts. And surely did indeed follow the pledges made in this book with regard to honoring wisdom.

Just consider the following text after God asked what Solomon wants:

"So give your servant a discerning heart to govern your people and to distinguish between right and wrong. For who is able to govern this great people of yours?" (1 Kings 3:4 NIV)

So we see that Solomon treasured wisdom. He could have asked the Supreme Being for virtually anything. But he asked God for wisdom.

This is what this text is about: It is about putting wisdom at the top of our goals when it comes to worldly achievements.

It is a lesson for all of us as we seek guidance in a confusing world.

The Wisdom of Solomon
Chapter One

1. If you love justice
you can judge the world.
Think of the Almighty with sincerity
and seek Him with a humble heart.

2. Because He is found
only by those who trust Him.
For He shows Himself
to those who have faith in Him.

3. For wicked thinking separates us
from God and His authority.
Such thinking condemns the unwise.

4. And wisdom penetrates not the malicious
nor will it dwell in a body
bound by wickedness.

5. Because the power of the Holy Spirit
departs from the deceitful
and withdraws from those
who judge without understanding.
He will not dwell
where dishonesty lies
and will depart from judgment
without understanding.

6. For the spirit of wisdom is benevolent.
It acquits not those who speak in wickedness
because God understands ones limits
for He knows the heart
and hears what is said.

7.   And the spirit of the Almighty
has filled the whole world
and that which contains everything
hears what is said.

8.   Thus those who speak wrongly
can never hide themselves
nor will they circumvent consequences
that will teach them.

9.   For unholy thinking gets examined
and every word we speak
is heard by God
and every action has consequences.

10. And the ear of envy hears so much
and the turmoil of rumor
cannot be hidden.

11. Therefore withdraw from rumor mongering
which will gain you nothing.
Refrain therefore from disparaging others
for loose lips have consequences
and lying lips harm the soul.

12. Seek not the ruin of error
within your lifetime
nor bring on destruction
through the works of your hands.

13. For God did not make ruination
nor does He pleasure
in the destruction of life.

14. He created all that has ever existed
and made the people of the earth
for their healing.
There is no venom of destruction

nor was earth created
to be a kingdom of hell.

15. For justice is perpetual
as well as immortal.

16. Yet with works and words
they bring on the wickedness
thinking it is a friend.
They join together with it
and make promises with it
because they became a part of it.

The Wisdom of Solomon Chapter Two

1.   They reason with themselves
and will say incorrectly:
"Life is short and difficult
and the end of a lifetime
brings no healing
and no one has ever been known
to have returned from hell.

2.   "For we are born from nothing
and after this we will not exist
and the breath in our nostrils is smoke
and speech is only a spark
to stir our emotions.

3.   "Once all is exhausted
our body will turn to ashes
and our spirit will pour out
into the surroundings like air.
And our life will pass
like the form of a cloud
and shall scatter like mist
dissolved by sunbeams
and evaporated by its heat.

4.   "In time our names will be forgotten
and no one will remember our deeds.

5.   "Because our time passes
just like a shadow
and there is no going back for us.
It is quickly shut down
and no one will return.

6. "Come therefore and we'll enjoy
the good things that are present
and let us quickly use
those around us as we did
when we were young.

7. "Let us fill ourselves
with expensive wines
and luxurious ointments
and we'll not let
the flower of time pass us by.

8. "Let us crown ourselves
with roses before they wither
and we'll not let any land
be absent of our parties.

9. "Let no one be without luxury
and let us savor
our moments of joy
for this is our portion
and this is our lot.

10. "Let us oppress the poor
nor will we spare the widows
nor honor the ancients
nor the graying hairs of the aged.

11. "But let our strength
be the rule of law
and that which is feeble
will be worth nothing.

12. "Let us therefore lie in wait
because those who are devoted
don't help our cause.
They oppose our deeds

and burden us down
with the heavy consequences
of our transgressions
and oppose the wickedness
of our way of life.

13. "They brag they know God
and call themselves God's servant.

14. "And now they censor our thoughts.

15. "They are angry at us
and yet looking at them
their life is not like others
and their ways are very different.

16. "They call us good for nothing
and detest our filthiness.
Yet they prefer consequences of justice
and glorify in God their Creator.

17. "Let's see if their words are true
and let's see what happens to them.
Then we will know
how it ends for them.

18. "For if they are the true servants of God
He will defend them
and will deliver them
from the hands of their enemies.

19. "Let's judge them
by his outrages and impunity
so we may know their humility
and try their patience.

20. "Let's condemn them
to a most shameful death

given the respect awarded to them
through their words."

21. They thought these things
and they were deceived.
They were blinded
by their own malice.

22. Yet they didn't know
about God's mysteries.
Nor did they hope for justice
or honor those holy souls.

23. For God created humans
to be trustworthy
and in His image
He made them.

24. But through the wickedness of envy
destruction entered the world.

25. But those who follow Him
are with Him.

The Wisdom of Solomon
Chapter Three

1. Yet trustworthy souls take shelter
within God's hands
so the traumas of destruction
do not touch them.

2. In the view of the ignorant
they may appear to die
and their departure can be
construed as miserable.

3. Yes their leaving us
is the ultimate destruction.
But they are in peace.

4. While they may appear to suffer
in the eyes of humans
their spirit is full of immortality.

5. They may be challenged sometimes
but mostly they are rewarded.
Because God has tested them
and found them worthy of trust.

6. Like gold from the furnace
He has screened them
and like victims of catastrophe
He hath received them.
Therefore with time
they will be honored.

7. The trustworthy will shine
and will shimmer like reflections
off the water between the reeds.

8. They may examine people
and govern over others
but the Almighty will reign forever.

9. Those who trust in Him
will understand the Truth.
And those who are faithful
in their love
will find rest in Him.
For those who chose Him
receive mercy and peace.

10. Yet the wicked receive consequences
according to their own devices.
They dishonor the holy
 and reject the Almighty.

11. For those who reject wisdom
become unhappy as a consequence.
Their goals are typically vain
and their labors find no fruit
and their works find no reward.

12. Their wives become unreasonable
and their children become hateful.

13. Their offspring become cursed
and satisfied with being barren.
Those not defiled
and haven't used the bed
for wicked acts
will be greeted by holy souls.

14. For even the castrate
who has not done harm
to others with deeds
nor considered wickedness

against God
the precious gift of faith
will be granted to them
and considered acceptable
in the temple of God.

15. For the fruit
of devoted works is glorious
and the root of wisdom
will never be pulled up.

16. And followers of perversion
cannot become perfect
and the seeds of wickedness
will become uprooted.

17. Should they live a long life
nothing will be achieved
and their last days
will be without honor.

18. Should they die sooner
they will find no hope
nor comforting speech
on the day of their hearing.

19. For despair results from wickedness.

The Wisdom of Solomon
Chapter Four

1.   Behold and praise the glory
of the devoted ones
because their remembrance elevates us
due to their service to God and others.

2.   Should the opportunity arrive
one may try to imitate them
and though it may impress others
and reap other benefits
and win over some conflicts
it cannot provide happiness.

3.   But the vast cult of wickedness
will never succeed
and impure activities
will gain no roots
and provide no solid foundation.

4.   While they may flourish
in some places for a while
because their position is not fastened
they will be shaken by winds
and the force of the winds
will cause their uproot.

5.   For their twisted branches
will break and their fruits
will be unprofitable
and sour to eat
and good for nothing.

6.   But followers of wicked seeds
become witnesses

against their leaders
in their judgment.

7.   But the devoted person
who is protected from death
shall be at peace.

8.   For the veneration of years
is not from the duration of time
nor counted by number of years.
A person's knowledge comes
with the grey hairs of experience.

8.   And a spotless life
becomes apparent
during the elderly years.

9.   Such a person pleased God
and was beloved
even while living among wickedness
they become transformed.

10. They rise above
despite the wickedness
that restricts knowledge
and deceit that harms the soul.

11. For the allurement of vanity
obscures goodness
and wandering desires
overwhelms an innocent mind.

13. Created perfectly in the short run
they are satisfied in the long run.

14. Because those souls please God
He quickly removes them
from the depths of abomination.

Yet many see this
and don't understand
nor do they retain these things
within their hearts.

15. For God's grace and mercy
belong to His devoted ones
and He honors those
who have chosen Him.

16. But those who are dead
will condemn the living.
Yet youth will also end
and soon become part
of the condemnation of lives.

17. They may see the demise
of a wise man
and not understand
what God designed for them
and why the Almighty
led them to safety.

18. They can see and despise them
but the Almighty will laugh
while they become embarrassed.

19. And they may fall afterward
without honor and blame
being dead forever.

20. But He will burst
their puffed up silent balloons.
This will shake them
from their very foundations
and lay them to waste
leaving them in sorrow
as they fade from memory.

20. They will come in fear
due to their wickedness.
And their abuses
will stand against them
and convict them.

The Wisdom of Solomon Chapter Five

1. The devoted will stand steadfast
against those who afflict them
and continue their work.

2. Those who understand this
will be amazed and awestruck
with their startling revelations.

3. They will apologize
and ask for mercy
praying for the release
of their spirit
even from those
who received criticism
and were derided
in a lesson of condemnation.

4. The fools value this world's madness
leaving an end without honor.

5. But just see how
the children of God
are considered worthy
just like the saints.

6. Those of us who have strayed
from the path of truth
will not have the light of justice
shining unto us
as the sun of knowledge
has not risen upon us.

7. We are worn by iniquity and destruction

after traveling our hardened paths
not knowing the way of the Almighty.

8.   What is gained through pride?
What benefits have come
from the esteem of our wealth?

9.   All those things pass away
like a branch that floats by.

10. Just as a ship passes
through the waves
when it has gone
no trace can be found
nor the path of its keel
seen through the waters.

11. Like a bird flying through the air
its passage leaves no mark found.
Only the sound of its wings
beating the light air
parting it by the flutter of her flight
she moves her wings
and flies on by
leaving no mark after her path.

12. Just as an arrow is shot at a mark
the divided air immediately comes together
again leaving the passage unknown.

13. Just as when we are born
immediately it is ended
and we are unable to show
any trace of virtue
being consumed by desire.

14. The wicked say these things
when they are in the material world.

15. But the desires of wickedness
are blown like dust in the wind.
Like a thin feather
drifting from a storm
like smoke scattered by wind
just as the memory of a foreigner
quickly passes by.

16. But the devoted live forever
their reward is with God
and their concerns
are with the Almighty.

17. Thus they receive
a glorious sanctuary
and a beautiful wreath
by the hand of the Almighty.
For with His right hand
He will shelter them
and with His holy arm
He will protect them.

18. And His pleasure
will become their armor
as He will arm the devoted
to fight off their enemies.

19. He will put on justice
like a breastplate
and wears pure judgment
instead of a helmet.

20. He will take charge
with an invincible shield:

20. And He will sharpen
his anger into a spear

and the whole world
shall fight with Him
against the unwise.

22. Then bolts of lightning
will descend from the clouds
like a bow that is taut
they shall be shot out
and will fly to the mark.

23. And thick hail will fall
on them from the stone
that casts with anger
the waters of the sea
which rage against them
and the rivers will run
a terrible course.

24. A mighty wind
will whip up against them
like a whirlwind
it will divide them
and their iniquity
shall turn earth into a desert
and wickedness shall overthrow
the thrones of the mighty.

The Wisdom of Solomon
Chapter Six

1. Wisdom is superior to strength
and a wise person
is superior to a strong person.

2. Therefore rulers please listen
and understand you judges
and learn to the ends of the earth.

3. Rulers of people listen
those given honor by many.

4. For power is granted to you
by the Almighty
and the authority of the Most High
will examine your actions
and understand your thoughts.

5. Because as ministers of His kingdom
you have not judged rightly
nor kept the law of justice
nor walked with the will of God.

6. Awesome and quick will He appear
for a most precise examination
shall be in store for them who rule.

7. For to those who are humble
mercy shall be given
but those who are confident
will be greatly challenged.

8. God will not exempt the soul
nor is He awed by human excellence.

For He made the humble and the great
and cares equally for them all.

9. So the greater challenges
will meet the more confident.

10. Therefore you authorities
listen to my words
so that you may learn wisdom
and not reject it and fall.

11. For those who keep righteousness
will become righteous
and those who have learned this
will have the answers.

12. Therefore hold fast to my words
and care for them
and you will receive guidance.

13. Wisdom is glorious
and never fades away.
She is easily seen
by those who love her
and she is easily found
by those who seek her.

14. She protects those who care for her
and shows herself first to them.

15. They who awaken early
to seek her out
will not be burdened
for they will find her
sitting at their door.

16. So thinking about her
perfects our understanding

and one that watches for her
will fast become secure.

17. For she will be worthy
of those who seek her
and she shows herself with joy
in ways and meet with providence.

18. For her the beginning
is the true meaning of discipline.

19. The focus of discipline is love
and love keeps her ways
and the keeping of her ways
is the foundation of righteousness.

20. For righteousness brings
us closer to God.

21. Thus wisdom delivers
the eternal sanctuary.

22. If you desire thrones and crowns
you rulers of people
then love wisdom
so you may reign for ever.

23. Love the light of wisdom
those with authority over others.

24. Know what wisdom is
and what caused her
and I declare this reveals
the mysteries of God.
So seek her out
from her beginnings
and deliver her knowledge
and gain the truth.

25. We should not consume envy
for such a person cannot
take part with wisdom.

26. Yet the multitude of the wise
is the welfare of the world
and the wise rulers
support their people.

27. Therefore receive the instruction
offered by these words
to offer you the benefits.

The Wisdom of Solomon
Chapter Seven

1. I am a mortal man
like everyone else
and my human race
was created from the earth
and in my mother's womb
My body formed from flesh.

2. In a period of ten months
was I trapped within blood
after coming from a man's seed
with the only comfort being sleep.

3. Once I was born
I breathed in the outside air
and fell upon the ground
from which I was made
and my first words
were said by crying
as do so many others.

4. I was nursed in diapers
and greatly cared for.

5. Yet none of the kings
experienced a birth differently.

6, For every human enters the same way
as they come into this world
just as they leave this world the same way.

7. So therefore I asked
and was given understanding
and I called upon God

and the spirit of wisdom came over me.

8.   Then I preferred her
more than kingdoms and thrones
and respectful wealth
nothing compares to her.

9.   Neither can I compare her
to any precious stone.
For all gold in comparison
is like a little sand
and silver held up to her
can be counted as clay.

10. I loved her greatly
above health and beauty
and chose her over light.
For her light can't be put out.

11. Now every good thing
has come with her
and uncountable wealth
has come through her hands.

12. So I rejoiced for all these
for it is wisdom that rises
for I knew not that she
was the mother of them all.

13. That I have learned innocently
and communicated without envy
as her wealth lays unhidden.

14. She is an infinite treasure
for those who use her
will become friends of God
graced with the gift of devotion.

15. So God let me speak
and then to be understanding
worthy of things given to me
because He is the guide of wisdom
and the director of the wise.

16. For we are all in His hands
and our words and wisdom
become the knowledge
that professes our works.

17. He has given me understanding
of the things we can know
like the nature of the universe
and the merits of the elements.

18. And the beginning and end
the trends of the times
the forks in the roads
and the changes of seasons.

19. The transformations of time
and the dispositions of the stars.

20. The personalities of animals
and the violence of wild beasts
the force of winds
and the reasoning of men
the diversities of plants
and the virtues of roots.

21. All these things are hidden
and are not foreseen.
I have learned from wisdom
the doer of all things
taught me.

22. For within her

is the spirit of understanding.
The Holy One
manifested and subtle
eloquent and active
undefiled and sure
sweet and loving
all that is good
quick yet never hindered
and beneficent.

23. Gentle and kind
steady, assured and secure
having all authority
overseeing everything
containing all spirits
intelligent, pure and subtle.

24. For wisdom is more active
than any active thing
and reaches everywhere
through her purity.

25. For she is the essence
of the power of God
a surely pure emanation
of the glory of the Almighty
and therefore nothing defiled
will affect her.

26. For she is the brightness
of the eternal light
and the unspotted mirror
of God's majesty
the image of His goodness.

27. Even though she is one
she can do everything.
Though she remains the same

she renews everything
and by the people
she conveys herself
into the souls of the holy
and she makes friends
of God and prophets.

28. For God loves those
within whom wisdom dwells.

29. For her beauty
eclipses the sun
above the order of stars
and just like light
she is found within.

30. After nighttime descends
wickedness never defeats wisdom.

The Wisdom of Solomon Chapter Eight

1. She expands her power
from one end to another
commanding all with nectar.

2. I have loved her
and have sought her out
since I was a kid
and wanted to marry her
such was my love
for her beauty.

3. She glorifies her nobility
with her connection to God.
Surely does the Almighty
have great love for her.

4. For she teaches knowledge
about the Supreme Being
and espouses His works.

5. And if riches are desired
what is richer than wisdom
which gives everything in life?

6. And if the senses are considered
who is a more artful performer
than she among these particulars?

7. And if someone loves justice
her work has great virtue
for she teaches justice and temperance
prudence and fortitude
which profit everyone in life.

8.   And if someone desires knowledge
she knows everything in the past
and makes judgment of things to come.
She knows the intricacies of speech
and the winners of debate.
She sees the signs and miracles
before they appear
and the events that span generations.

9.   I am committed to bring her
with me throughout my life
knowing she keeps me informed
and comforts me
during times of grief.

10. Because of her
I will be praised by others
and honored by the ancient ones
despite my youth.

11. Thus will I have a means
to swiftly make good judgment
and please those in power
and therefore I will receive
the blessings of princes.

12. They will await my pause
and look to me to speak
and will be surprised
should I speak in detail.

13. It is therefore by her grace
that I will have immortality
and leave behind a memory
for those who come after me.

14. And I shall provide an example

for other people who honor me.

The Wisdom of Solomon
Chapter Nine

1. Then the unbelievers will say
as they reason with themselves
yet not correctly:
"Our life is short and tiresome
and when a human dies
there is no remedy
nor has there been anyone
known to return from death.

2. "For we are all born
as an experience
and we will therefore
live as though we never existed
because the air in our lungs
is like smoke sparked
from the movement of our heart.

3. "Then after being pushed out
our body will turn to ashes
and our spirit will vanish
like a breeze in the air.

4. "We will be forgotten in time
no one will remember our deeds
and we will pass away
just as the trace of a cloud
to be dispersed as moisture
and evaporated by sun beams
that accompany its heat.

5. "Our days are like a passing shadow
from which there is no return
for it is quickly gone

so no one can come again.

6. "So let's just move along
and enjoy the good things in life
and quickly do was we did as kids.

7. "Let's fill ourselves up
on expensive wines and incense
leaving no spring flowers untouched.

8. "Let's adorn ourselves
with bouquets of roses
before they become withered.

9. "We will continue our vanity
and leave behind everywhere
tokens of our desires
for this is our condition
and this is our allotment.

10. "We oppress the innocent poor
and we won't spare the widows
nor will we honor the elderly.

11. "Our strength will be the law
otherwise there is no worth in weakness.

12. "Therefore we will lie in wait
for those who are righteous
for they look out for us not
and clean up despite our activities.
But they challenged us
and offended our laws
and objected to our positions
disregarding our education.

13. "They profess a knowledge of God
calling themselves servants of the Almighty.

14. "They were created
to criticize our thinking.

15. "They are hard to look at
for their life is not like others
and their ways are different.

16. "We honor them as impersonators
they avoid us like we are dirty
and predict the demise of the just
just to become blessed
boasting that God is their Creator.

17. "Let us see if their words are honest
and we will see what will happen
when their end arrives.

18. "For if a just person
is the servant of God
He will help them
and deliver them
from the hands of their enemies.

19. "Let's watch them carefully
so we can understand their humility
and see how long they will last.

21. "Let's punish them
with a shameful death
for their words will honor Him."

21. These are what they imagined
but they were deceived
for their wickedness blinded them.

22. For they knew not
the mysteries of God

nor did they wish
for righteous work
nor did they seek
the consequences of innocence.

23. For God created souls as immortal
and He made them in His image
for all of eternity.

24. But from self-centered envy
entered death into the universe
and those who take hold of it
will indeed find it.

The Wisdom of Solomon
Chapter Ten

1.   She protected the first ancestors
within the world created
and delivered from their downfall.

2.   Then she gave them the authority
to be caretakers of everything.

3.   But through wickedness they left her
and with their anger
they perished in their hatred
and murdered the brother.

4.   This eventually was the cause
for the earth to be flooded
but wisdom was still preserved
which directed the paths
for the righteous
within a small core of morality.

5.   Even though the peoples
were wrapped within their wickedness
she sought out the righteous
and protected their innocence before God
and strengthened them with compassion
suitable for His servants.

6.   As the wicked died
she delivered the righteous
who fled from the fire
that fell down on the five cities.

7.   Those whose wickedness
laid waste on the land

which smokes with testimony
and plants bearing fruit
that never get ripe
and a pillar of salt standing
as a monument for unbelieving souls.

8.   For without wisdom
they receive not just the pain
from the things they knew not
but those that were good
yet also left behind
in the world as a memorial
of their foolishness
so the things they offended
could not be hidden.

9.   But wisdom delivered from suffering
those who attended to her.

10. When the righteous escaped
from their brother's wrath
she guided them to right paths
and showed them God's sanctuary
and gave them spiritual knowledge
to make their journeys fruitful
by multiplying the fruits
of their various endeavors.

11. For through the envy
of those who oppressed them
she stood by them
and rewarded them greatly.

12. She defended them from enemies
and kept them safe
from those who hid in waiting
and in devastating conflict
she gave them victory

so they might realize
that goodness is stronger.

13. When the righteous were disposed of
she did not forsake them
but delivered them from wickedness
and pulled them out from the pit.

14. And she untied their bonds
and brought them the sanctuary
and strength against their oppressors
for those who had accused them
she showed them to be liars
and gave them eternal honor.

15. She delivered the righteous
and their innocent offspring
from those who oppressed them.

16. She entered the soul
of the servant of the Almighty
to withstand wicked rulers
and their miracles and signs.

17. Giving the righteous rewards
as a result of their endeavors
and providing wonderful guidance
by giving them shelter by day
and the lights of stars by night.

18. Bringing them through the Red Sea
and leading them through deep waters.

19. And she drowned their enemies
by laying them down in the depths.

20. Thus the righteous spoiled the ungodly
by praising the Name of the Almighty

and laying upon them Your hand
which had fought for them.

23. For wisdom opens
the mouth of the dumb
and makes tongues for those
who cannot speak eloquently.

The Wisdom of Solomon
Chapter Eleven

1. She advances their activities
through the means of Holy Prophets.

2. They travel through the wilderness
which had not been barren
and pitched tents in places
off of the beaten path.

3. They stood against their adversaries
and avenged their challengers.

4. When thirsty they called on You
and water came from rock shale
and their thirst was quenched
from the hard stone.

5. Because the same things
that punished their adversaries
provided benefits for them.

6. Instead of a river that ran
polluted with foul blood.

7. Instead of disavowing
any particular instruction
ending with infants being killed
You gave them water aplenty
when they ran out of hope.

8. They declared with haste
that You overcame their challenges.

9. Because they desired mercy

they knew also how the wicked
were condemned by consequence
by desiring the opposite
of what the righteous wanted.

10. For they were reprimanded
just as a father might
and just like a harsh ruler
they have suffered the consequences.

11. Whether here or away
they were still confused.

12. For a twofold sadness came over them
with a cry for the memory
of the things of the past.

13. And when they understood
through consequences experienced
wherein lies the benefits
they opened their hearts
up to the Almighty.

14. To those they gave disdain
long after they were rejected
as the infants were cast out
at the end of it all
when they understood
what came to pass
they felt admiration.

15. Yet the means of wickedness
which they used to deceive
and honored snakes
that were void of reason
along with violent beasts
You sent a multitude
of unreasonable beasts

to teach them by consequence.

16. The meaning is revealed
that when someone harms another
so shall they be harmed.

17. It was Your Almighty hand
that made the world of matter from nothing
without seeking the means
to attack with bears or fierce lions.

18. Similarly with other wild beasts
complete with fury from birth
breathing fire and smoke
stinking of filth
shooting spikes from their eyes.

19. Not only the risk of harm
that could come upon them
along with the horrible sighting
that would terrify them.

20. Yes they may have fallen down
with only one blow
being punished by consequence
and scattered through the land
blown down by Your power
just as You have ordained
everything in good measure
in number and weight.

21. For You can show
Your great strength anytime
only when You want to
but how could anyone withstand
the power of Your arm?

22. For the entire world

is but a little grain in the balance
just as a drop of morning dew
that falls down on the earth.

23. Yet You caste mercy upon all
for You can do anything
and wink at human transgressions
because they can be amended.

24. For You care for everything
and abhor nothing You have made
for never would You have made
anything You didn't want to.

25. And how could anything continue
if not for Your will?
Or anything have been preserved
if You had not called upon it?

26. But You deliver them all
for they are Yours Almighty
You lover of souls.

The Wisdom of Solomon
Chapter Twelve

1. For Your imperishable Spirit
is contained within everything.

2. Therefore You gradually teach
those who are offensive
and You remind them
that they can depart wickedness
and can trust in You the Almighty.

3. For it was by Your will
that descendants defeated
those ancient inhabitants
of Your holy land.

4. You abhorred them
for they were doing wicked things
and making wicked sacrifices.

5. As well as murdering children
without any mercy.
They ate human flesh
and had feasts of blood.

6. Their priests stood by
as they made offerings
to idols and ancestors
and with their own hands
murdered those souls
without mercy.

7. But this earth
which some hold dear
above everything else

could very well sustain
an esteemed generation
devoted to God.

8.   Yet even those humans
whom You had protected
were met with wasps
the forerunners of Your host
to weaken them over time.

9.   Not that the wasps
could deliver the wicked
back into the hands
of the righteous in battle
nor could destroy them
suddenly with hostile beasts
or with one harsh word.

10. But by giving to them
Your instructions over time
You gave them a place to repent
knowing they were wicked
and their malice was inherited
and their mindset unchanged.

11. For it was a cursed generation
from the beginning.
Nor were You compelled
to give them pardons
for those wicked things
that they had done.

12. For who could question
What You have done?
Who could understand your decisions?
Who shall accuse you
for those who perish
and those You created?

And who could stand against You
and be repaid for the wicked?

13. For there is no God but You
who cares for everyone
to whom You might show
that Your judgment is right.

14. Nor can a king or tyrant
be able to challenge You
or those receiving consequences.

15. Because You are righteous
You implement everything righteously.
For Your authority is independent
from using Your authority
to condemn someone
not deserving punishment.

16. For Your authority provides
the foundation of righteousness
and because You are the Almighty
You are merciful to all.

17. To those who don't believe
that You are in control
You show your strength.
And for those that already know this
You give them strength.

18. Yet You are in control
and decides with fairness
to give us instructions
with great pleasure
so You can use Your power
whenever You want.

19. Yet by these deeds

You have taught Your people
that the righteous are merciful
and have given Your followers
confidence that You will
forgive their wickedness.

20. You could have punished
the enemies of Your devoted ones
and condemned them to death
with a harsh judgment.
Yet You give them time
and the opportunity
to turn their lives around
and correct their ways.

21. With such great circumspection
have You judged Your devoted
after You committed to their teachers
and made promises of Your sanctuary.

22. Thus You have embraced us
and defeated our enemies
at least a thousand times
to the extent that we determine
as we consider Your goodness
so that when we are judged
we can receive Your mercy.

23. Yet when people live wickedly
they are meet with consequences
for their own wicked activities.

24. As they stray off
towards the wrong path
and embrace their gods
even the beasts of their enemies
are despised and deceived
like innocent and ignorant children.

25. Those unreasonable children
are met by the consequences
of their own derision.

26. But those who are unhindered
can be given some grace
to give them fairness from God.

27. For those things they despise
as they suffer the consequences
become whom they thought as gods
now they are being punished.
So when they saw these things
they acknowledged God as true
whom they denied knowing before
thus condemning themselves.

The Wisdom of Solomon
Chapter Thirteen

1.   By nature humans are egotistical
and do not know God
and from the things that are seen
they cannot know Him
nor from understanding events
can they know who is Master.

2.   But whether by fire or wind
or a stormy wind
or the dome of stars
or the rushing water
the gods that govern this world

3.   Due to their beauty and delight
they understood them to be gods.
Let them know how much
better the Lord of them is
for the original Creator of beauty
did indeed create them.

4.   If they were astonished
at their power and virtue
let us understand
how much mightier
He who created them is.

5.   For by the greatness and beauty
relative to the creatures
their Creator is perceived.

6.   There is therefore no blame
for those who err in their ways
as they seek God

being desirous to find Him.

7.   People carefully search for Him
because they know His actions
and believe what they see
because His creations are beautiful.

8.   Yet they may never find mercy.

9.   For if they knew so much
they could search the world
and still they could not
find the Almighty there?

10. But they remain in misery
as their hope is in dead things
and they call them gods
though they are human made
even in gold and silver
and shown as art
resembling beasts or stone
but they are good for nothing
and works of ancient hands.

11. The wood workers saw a tree
that would work for the task
after taking off all the bark
with significant skill
chiseled it beautifully
and made a vessel from it
ready for the service of someone.

12. And after expending
the remainder of their efforts
to feed themselves
they have completed it.

13. Then working on a piece

of that which served no one
taken from crooked wood
that was full of knots
they carved it diligently
when they had nothing else to do
forming it though their skill
fashioning an image of a human.

14. Or they carved it like
some hostile creature
laying it over with red paint
and covering all the spots.

15. Then they made an access room
and set it into a wall
and fastened it with iron.

16. Thus they installed it such
that it would not fall over
understanding it could not help itself
because after all it was an image
in need of assistance.

17. Then they prayed for things
for their wife and children
and were not ashamed
to speak to something dead.

18. To heal they called on weakness
to live they prayed to the dead
for aid they humbly called upon
those with the least ability to help.
And asked for their safe journeys
from that who never traveled.

19. Then to achieve their results
and succeed in their work
they asked that from which

had no ability to do anything.

The Wisdom of Solomon Chapter Fourteen

1. Should someone preparing to sail
preparing to transverse raging seas
call on a piece of wood
more rotten than the boat
that will carry them?

2. Surely it was desire for gain
that motivated its making
by the wood worker who built it
through his skill.

3. Yet it is through providence
by the control of the Almighty
that has led you to the sea
and provided a safe path
through the waves.

4. Showing that one is saved
from all types of danger
even one who went to sea
without the skill to do so.

5. Even if Your wisdom
is not utilized
and some commit their lives
to a small piece of wood
and sail through rough seas
in a weak vessel
many still are saved.

6. For in the ancient times
when the proud giants perished
worldly dreams guided by You

did escape in weak vessels
leaving their offspring
to the coming ages.

7.   For blessed is the wood
from which righteousness comes.

8.   But cursed is that which
is made with hands
because those who made them
are themselves flawed
even if they are called god.

9.   For the ungodly and ungodliness
are similarly opposed to God.

10. And those who do these
shall face consequences together
with those who made them.

11. Therefore even the idols
of the atheists are visited
because within the world of God
they have become an abomination
and have become stumbling blocks
to the souls of people
and have become snares
to the soles of the unwise.

12. For the production of idols
began a spiritual impunity
and their invention
was a corruption of life.

13. And neither did they exist
from the beginning
nor do they last for ever.

14. Only by the vanity of people
did they come into the world
and thus met with a swift end.

15. Like a father afflicted
with an untimely passing
and the image of his child
was quickly taken away
only to be honored as a god
even though a dead man
and delivered to others
which came after him
for rituals and sacrifices.

16. In time this unseemly custom
grew strong and written into law.
So engraved images were worshipped
through the instructions of kings.

17. Those who didn't receive honor
because they lived too far away
were considered imitation effigies
to make a discrete image of a ruler
who then received their honor.
For this they received nobility
by flattering those that were absent
as if they were present.

18. But due to their persistent fraud
they produced more ignorance
because of heightened superstition.

19. For those who were willing
to please those with authority
were forced to use their skills
to make effigies of great quality.

20. Thus those who were attracted

by the beauty of the effigies
mistook them to be gods
while only just a little before
had received honor.

21. And this deceives the world
to those who serve disaster
and subscribe to stones
ascribed by unspoken names.

22. Yet this was insufficient
due to misunderstandings of God
because they took residence
in the great battle of ignorance
against the great plagues of peace.

23. While they killed their children
in sacrifices and secret ceremonies
or reveled during strange rituals

24. They neglected lives and marriages
and killed one another without valor
or offended them with infidelity.

25. This ruled over the people
causing murder and manslaughter
theft and deception
corruption and lying
violence and perjury.

26. This led to distress of good people
forgetfulness of good deeds
defiling of the spiritual person
changing of the types
discord among marriages
adultery and brazen impurity.

27. Thus the worship of unnamed idols

is the beginning and the cause
and the end of all wickedness.

28. For either are they crazy
when they are merry
or their prophesy lies
or they live dishonorably
or they simply abandon themselves.

29. Because they trust in idols
which are not alive
even if they swear falsehoods
they seem to have no damage.

30. They shall suffer the consequences
not only for despising God
but for following idols
and wickedly swearing
deceiving and despising holiness.

31. For they do not swear
by their own power.
It is the vengeance of the wicked
and their eventual consequences
that provides offences for the ungodly.

The Wisdom of Solomon
Chapter Fifteen

1. Yet God You are kind and pure
patient and merciful
and in control of all things.

2. We are Yours even if we sin
because we know Your power
yet we are not wicked
because we know we are Yours.

3. For to know You
is the perfection of righteousness
to know Your power
is the root of immortality.

4. The deception of humanity
deceived us not
just as a colorful painting
illustrates a painter's tireless effort.

5. Such sights temp fools
who lust for them
desiring the form of a dead image
which has no breath.

6. Those who make them
and those who desire them
and those who worship them
are all lovers of wickedness
and thus are worthy
to trust of such things.

7. Now the potter
molds the softened earth

to fashion every cup
with their hard work
and yet the same clay
can be used also for
cleaning containers
and things for service
but regardless of the product
the potter makes the decision.

8.   Employing talents without shame
making a vanity god the same day
though it was earth just before
and just after will return to the same
just as their body that was lent
will be demanded back.

9.   Yet their major care is not
how much work they have to do
or that is life is so short
but strives to better the work
of goldsmiths and silversmiths
as they seek to work in brass
while being proud of themselves
for making counterfeit things.

10. Their hearts become ashes
and their hope more vile than dirt
as their life has less value than mud.

11. Because they didn't know their Creator
Who breathed life into them
and inspired an active soul.

12. Yet they figured their life a pastime
and our time here a market for gain
for they say we must grab everything
even if it be by wicked means.

13. For the materialistic person
who makes breakable vessels
and images that are dead
knowingly offends all others.

14. The oppressors of Your people
who keep them in bondage
are the most foolish
and more miserable than newborns.

15. Because they assumed idols
of the deluded were gods
though they have no eyes to see
nor noses to draw breath
nor ears to hear
nor fingers to handle
with feet not meant to travel.

16. Because humans made them
carved with borrowed spirit
unable to make a god in their likeness.

17. Because they are mortal
they made something dead
with wicked hands
but they themselves are better
than those things they worship
for they only live for a time
but what they made never lives.

18. Yes they worshiped beasts
that are certainly also hateful
and as they are compared
some are worse than others.

19. Nor are they beautiful
which is typical of beasts
acting without God's blessings.

The Wisdom of Solomon
Chapter Sixteen

1. They face their consequences
tormented by many creatures.

2.   Outside of this process
You deal graciously
with Your followers
facilitating exotic foods for them
those that even quails may discover.

3.   So when they desire food
they may seek out those beasts
which they caution against
but when they desire this
and suffer scarcity sometimes
they may partake of exotic foods.

4.   For this may be necessary
for tyranny is unavoidably consequential
but they would only serve to show
that their adversaries have suffered.

5.   Because the terror of beasts
were upon them
they perished from the stings
of vicious snakes
a wrath of temporary effect.

6.   Yet they were anxious for a time
that they might be admonished
and given the sign of redemption
in order for them to remember
the instructions given by You.

7. For those who turned towards it
were not saved by what was seen
but rather by You
because You are everyone's Savior.

8. And by doing this
Your adversaries confess
that it is You
who delivers us from wickedness.

9. Even after they were bit by insects
they did not find a cure for their life
thus they had to face those consequences.

10. But Your followers overcame
not by the bite of snakes
but Your mercy were they healed
which never left them.

11. They were encouraged
to remember Your instructions
and were immediately restored
and prevented from forgetfulness
allowing them to understand Your goodness.

12. For it was neither medicinal herb
nor soothing balm
that restored them to health
but rather Your word O Lord
which heals all things.

13. You have authority
over life and death.
You can lead one
to the gates of hell
and lift them up again.

14. Someone who kills using hostility
like a spirit that goes forth
will not return
just as the soul received
will come back again.

15. Still it is not possible
to escape from Your hand.

16. Because the wicked
who decided to ignore You
were decimated
by Your power
with hard rains, hail and showers
did they suffer
and they couldn't avoid
the fire they consumed.

17. What is truly astounding
is the fire overpowered the water
which will quench everything
and the world fights for the righteous.

18. For sometimes the flame burnt out
so it wouldn't burn those warriors
sent against the atheists
but themselves will understand
that they faced the consequences
by the judgment of God.

19. Then another time it did burn
even within the water
above the power of fire
so that it destroyed
the fruits of an unjust land.

20 Instead You fed Your people
with manna from heaven

prepared with love
able to fulfill every one
delightful and agreeable to all tastes.

21. For it is Your sustenance
that provides sweetness to Your children
by serving to satisfy their appetite
and designed to please every person.

22. Yet snow and ice endures the fire
and doesn't melt
so they might know
that fire burns within the hail
and sparks in the rain
to destroy the fruits of the adversaries.

23. But even this did not negate
His power to provide
nourishment to the righteous.

24. For those who serve You
the Creator's authority over the wicked
leads to their consequences
while yielding for the benefit
of those who put their trust in You.

25. Thus even as they changed
in so many ways
becoming obedient to Your grace
which nourishes all things
according to their desires
in their time of need.

26. So Lord Your children
whom You love
will know that fruits
do not nourish the soul
but it is Your word

that preserves those
who put their trust in You.

27. For what isn't destroyed by fire
after warming from the sun's rays
will soon melt away.

28. In order to let this be known
we give You thanks before the sun
and pray to you till daybreak.

29. For the wishes of the unappreciated
melt away with the winter's first frost
and run off like unneeded water.

The Wisdom of Solomon
Chapter Seventeen

1. Your decisions are perfect
beyond all comprehension
thus uneducated souls are mistaken.

2. Because wicked people
seek to oppress holy people
they become trapped in their houses
becoming prisoners of darkness
captive for a long night of bondage
and banished from their eternal destination.

3. While they assumed a lie
hiding within wicked secrecy
they became scattered
within the dark veil of forgetfulness
being horribly astonished
troubled by strange apparitions.

4. While none of the corners
that kept them from their fears
like the noise of waters falling
down all around them
and sad visions appeared
to them with heavy features.

5. The force of fire gave them no light
nor could the brightness of the stars
last to give light to that horrible night.

6. Just the dreadful appearance
of a fire started on its own

which was terrifying
did they think those things they saw
were worse than not seeing.

7. With the illusions of the dark arts
they were smothered out
and the wisdom they flaunted
was rebuked in disgrace.

8. For those who promised
to drive away the fears
and the anxiety of a sick soul
were beside themselves with fear
and worthy of ridicule.

9. Though no beast feared them
they were scared by passing animals
and the hissing of snakes.

10. Their fear left them lifeless
disregarding their visions in the sky
which provided no ability to ignore.

11. Thus wickedness was condemned
by her own frightened witness
being pressured by conscience
and predicting future disasters.

12. For fear is nothing else
but an abandonment of comfort
that is offered by reason.

13. And the humble hope from within
counts ignorance more than cause
which brings about the torment.

14. But they slept the same that night
but it was certainly intolerable

arriving from the depths of darkness.

15. Being disturbed by horrific apparitions
and fainting with failing hearts
as an unseen and unexpected fear
at once arose within them.

16. Thus when they fell
they fell straight down
and were locked in a prison
that had no iron bars.

17. Whether husbandman or shepherd
or laborer out in the field
all were caught off guard
and sustained the necessity
that could not be avoided
because they were all bound
on one chain of darkness.

18. Whether from a whistling wind
or a melodious noise of birds
spreading along the branches
or the fall of water
rushing down wildly.

19. Or the dreadful sound
of stones falling down
or a running unseen by trotting animals
or the roar of savage wild beasts
or the resounding echo off mountain valleys
these made them swoon with fear.

20. For the entire world glowed
in the clearest of light
with none hindered by their work.

21. Over them the dark night spread

with the image of darkness
that would receive them afterwards
being more heinous than darkness.

The Wisdom of Solomon
Chapter Eighteen

1. As Your servants shine bright
their voices will be heard
even without being seen
they don't suffer those things
because they are satisfied within.

2. As for those who didn't hurt them
those who had been wronged earlier
extend their gratitude to them
and seek their forgiveness
even though they had been enemies.

3. Rather You gave them a burning pillar
as both a guide for an uncertain journey
and a harmless sun
to entertain their honor

4. They wanted to be deprived of light
and imprisoned by darkness
after incarcerating Your servants
from whom came the light
of uncorrupted justice
given unto the world.

5. When they decided to murder
the babes of the saints
a child was delivered
in order to rebuke them
thus many of their children were taken
and ruined in a mighty flood.

6. That night our ancestors were justified

for accepting those promises
on which they put their trust
giving them a sustained relief.

7.   Acceptance among Your people
included salvation for the righteous
and the destruction of their enemies.

8.   Because You rebuked those against us
You also glorified those of us
whom You had called upon.

9.   For the righteous followers
of the just people
secretly sacrificed themselves
and made a holy promise
to join together with the saints
through goodness and wickedness
which the ancients now sing about
with their songs of praise.

10. But ill will arose from others
who cried out their opposition
with tears of lamentation
traveling through the land
for the followers who spoke out.

11. Both master and servant
suffered those consequences
and kings and common people
suffered alike.

12. They all died together
countless passed away at once
and none were alive enough
to bury the dead
for within one moment
even the noblest descendents

among them were annihilated.

13. For they just would not believe
until the miracles appeared
and after destruction of the firstborn
they did acknowledge these people
were the followers of God.

14. Everywhere there is silence
and the night covered everything.

15. But the word of the Almighty
descended from the spiritual realm
from Your exalted sanctuary
like a fierce warrior
within a place of destruction.

16. You delivered Your pure wisdom
like a sharp sword
that stood up against death
by touching the spiritual realm
while standing upon the earth.

17. Suddenly visions of horrible dreams
troubled them deeply
and the terrors shocked them.

18. Yet the half dead were thrown here
and some were thrown there
illustrating the nature of their death.

19. And their troubling dreams
indeed did predict this
and they perished without knowing
what caused their afflictions.

20. Yes the taste of death
does also touch the righteous

while others faced destruction
within the wilderness
yet the wrath did not endure.

21. For the innocents reacted fast
and stood up to defend them
bringing the shield of His ministry
with prayers and offerings
prepared themselves for the challenges
in order to end the destruction
declaring they were Your servants.

22. Thus they overcame the destroyer
not with strength of the body
nor by the force of weapons
but with a word subdued the punishers
by proclaiming the promises
and agreements made with the ancestors.

23. When the dead fell around them
piled up one upon another in great piles
He resisted the destruction
and parted the way to the living.

24. That area contained the universe
and the four rows of its stones
were engraved with their glory
and the crowns on their heads
contained Your Majesty.

25. The opposers gave way to them
and were afraid of them
because they had enough
of the taste of their strength.

The Wisdom of Solomon Chapter Nineteen

1. As for the ungodly
their end came upon them
with out any mercy
because they knew before
what would happen to them.

2. Now they permitted them to leave
and quickly sent them away
but they changed their minds
and began to pursue them.

3. Because even while they mourned
and lamented at the graves
they made another mistake
and pursued them like fugitives
though they allowed them to leave.

4. They were worthy of their fate
which drew them to this result
and made them forget those things
that had happened beforehand
so the consequences they feared
would indeed be fulfilled.

5. While Your followers could leave
in such an appropriate manner
they were met with unexpected death.

6. Because the reality of the whole
became newly modeled once again
serving the specific instructions
which were given unto them

so Your children were protected.

7.   As this occurred a cloud hovered above
and where there was water
dry land suddenly rose up
and out from the Red Sea
a clear path was revealed
and from the raging waves
came a green field.

8.   Through this went the people
whom You protected with Your hand
through Your wonderful surprises.

9.   They ran through as on horses
and leaping as lambs
and they praised You Lord
You who had delivered them.

10. Because they knew the things
done during their journey
through the foreign land
when flies rose from the ground
instead of the cows
and frogs rose from the river
instead of the fishes.

11. Afterward they saw new flocks of birds
that led them with their appetite
as they searched for favorable foods.

12. For quails came to them
from the sea for their satisfaction.

13. And the consequences of the wicked
who were given signs
through the power of thunder
they suffered justice

according to their own wickedness
because of their hardness
and hateful behavior towards others.

14. Because Sodomites didn't welcome them
and didn't recognize them as they came
they brought them into bondage
just as they had deserved.

15. Then the chance of respect
would be taken by them
because they used hostile foreigners.

16. Then they were wounded badly
by those they had celebrated
and had shared with them
the same set of codes.

17. Thus even those who were blind
were stricken just the same
as those becoming righteous
with fear of the terrifying darkness
seeking departure through their doors.

18. Because the elements rearranged
through a type of harmony
just as the notes of a song
can change the nature of a tune
while all are still sounds
having seen those things
which had taken place.

19. For solids turned to fluids
and creatures that once swam
now traversed the ground.

20. The fire had power over water
forgetting its own stature

and the water had forgotten
its own quenching nature.

21. On the opposing side
those flames burned not the flesh
of those innocent living beings
though walking through it
and those of the cold depths
didn't heat or melt
though the sky was hot
normally enough to burn them.

22. In all You do Almighty Lord
You glorify Your devoted ones
and You take them not for granted
but You protect them
every time and every place.

Made in the USA
Monee, IL
09 April 2024

56696714R00049